BEAGLES

FAVORITE DOG BREEDS

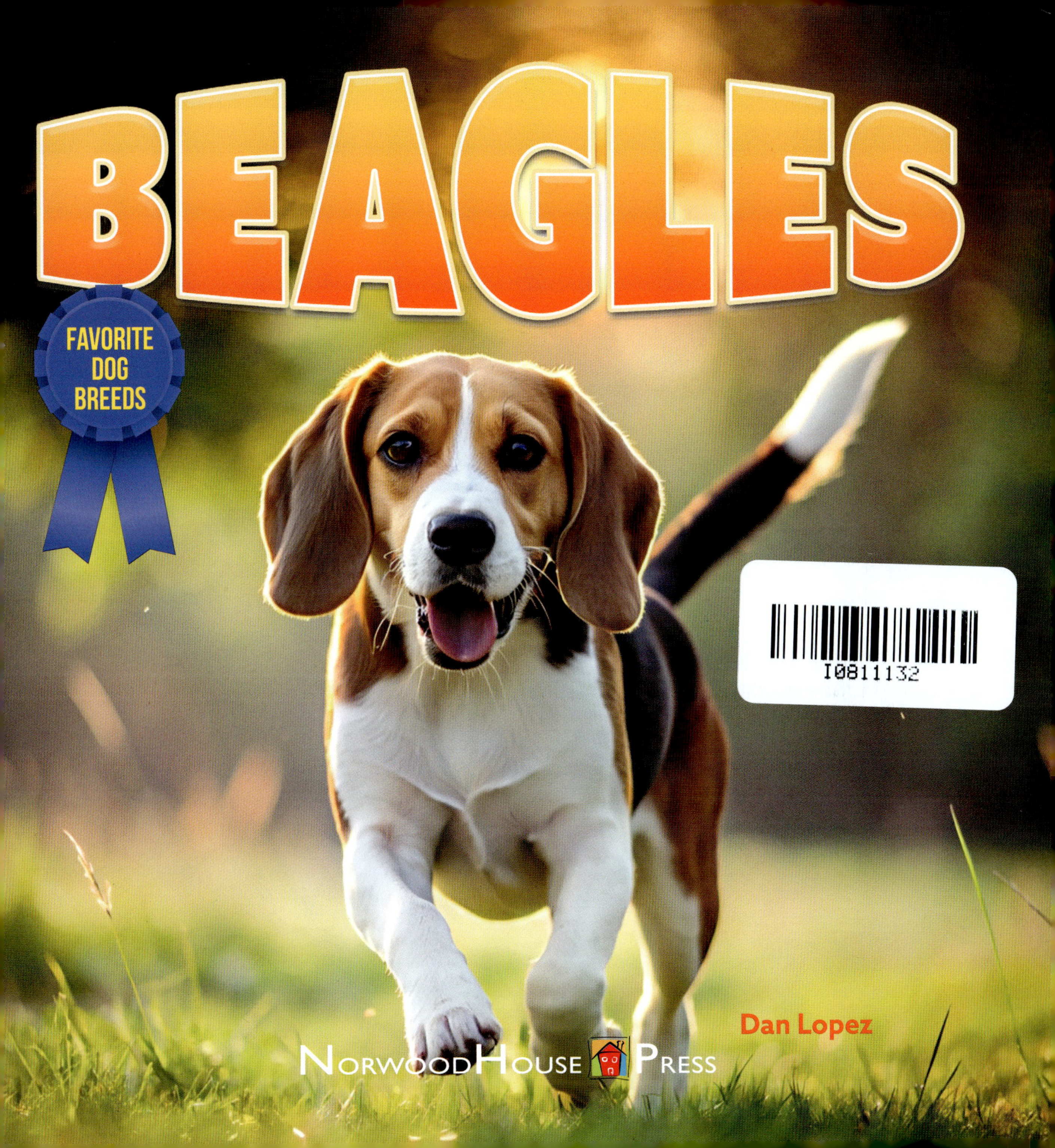

Dan Lopez

NorwoodHouse Press

Cataloging-in-Publication Data

Names: Lopez, Dan.
Title: Beagles / Dan Lopez.
Description: Buffalo, NY : Norwood House Press, 2026. | Series: Favorite dog breeds| Includes glossary and index.
Identifiers: ISBN 9781978576506 (pbk.) | ISBN 9781978576513 (library bound) | ISBN 9781978576520 (ebook)
Subjects: LCSH: Beagle (Dog breed)--Juvenile literature.
Classification: LCC SF429.B3 L67 2026 | DDC 636.7537--dc23

Published in 2026 by
Norwood House Press
2544 Clinton Street
Buffalo, NY 14224

Designer: Rhea Magaro
Editor: Kim Thompson

Photo credits: Cover, p. 16 michael_coelho, Giraphics/Shutterstock.com; p. 4 Shutterstock AI/Shutterstock.com; p. 5 Stock Holm/Shutterstock.com; p. 6 Igor Normann/Shutterstock.com; p. 9 Sigma_S/Shutterstock.com; p. 10 Ignacy Sedlak/Shutterstock.com; p. 11 Kim Dubois/Shutterstock.com; p. 13 Yavdat/Shutterstock.com; p. 14 Hedley Lamarr/Shutterstock.com; p. 16 Natalia Anyukhina/Shutterstock.com; p. 17 Lunja/Shutterstock.com; p. 19 PixieMe/Shutterstock.com; p. 20 Przemek Iciak/Shutterstock.com; p. 21 Joseph Jacobs/Shutterstock.com

Printed in the United States of America

CPSIA compliance information: Batch #CWNHP26: For further information contact Norwood House Press at 1-800-237-9932.

TABLE OF CONTENTS

Meet the Beagle

Beagles are popular pets. Dogs of this **breed** are known for having floppy ears, **sensitive** noses, and **outgoing** personalities.

The most famous beagle is the *Peanuts* character Snoopy.

What Do Beagles Look Like?

Beagles are medium-sized dogs with large eyes and long ears. When a beagle lowers its **snout**, its ears dangle close to the ground. This helps funnel **scents** toward the dog's nose.

Beagles have short **coats** that do not need a lot of grooming. Their fur has patches of white, tan, brown, and black. They can even have freckles.

There are two types of beagles: small and large. A small beagle measures less than 13 inches (33 centimeters) tall at the shoulder. Large beagles are about 15 inches (38 centimeters) tall at the shoulder.

Beagles weigh 20 pounds (nine kilograms) or more.

Where Do Beagles Come From?

Beagles are ancient dogs. They have been **companions** to people for thousands of years. *Beagle* may come from the French word *begueule,* which means “loudmouth.”

Long ago, **packs** of beagles helped hunters find animals. With their talented noses held close to the ground, beagles are excellent **trackers**. They like to snoop and explore.

Do Beagles Make Good Pets?

Beagles make great pets. They are friendly to people and to other dogs.

Beagles are full of energy. They love to play outside.

Beagles will bark loudly to protect their homes. Their howls might wake sleeping babies or bother neighbors.

What Do Beagles Need?

Plenty of exercise keeps beagles from getting bored. They need to be active for at least an hour each day.

If beagles smell something interesting, they may roam away. They need to be **confined** inside or in a fenced yard.

Glossary

breed (breed): one type or kind of an animal

coats (kohts): the hair or fur that covers animals' bodies

companions (kuhm-PAN-yuhnz): friends, buddies, or partners

confined (kuhn-FINED): kept in a limited space; not allowed to wander freely

outgoing (OUT-goh-ing): friendly and eager to meet new people

packs (paks): groups of animals that live and hunt together

scents (sents): smells

sensitive (SEN-si-tiv): able to notice or feel things easily

snout (snout): the long front part of an animal's head that includes the nose and mouth

trackers (TRAK-urz): animals that are good at finding things by following trails left behind on the ground

Thinking Questions

1. Describe a beagle's coat.
2. Describe a beagle's personality.
3. How do a beagle's ears help it smell?
4. How can beagles help hunters?
5. Why do beagles need to be confined?

Index

About the Author

Dan Lopez is a writer who loves dogs! He has a German shepherd named Hans and an Irish setter named Tam. They love to go for walks in the woods together. Sometimes, they jump in the lake for a swim. Dan lives in Indiana with his wife and three kids.